LOVE AT THE FULL

for Sylvia

LOVE AT THE FULL

Lucien Becker

A translation of *Plein Amour*

by Christopher Pilling

FLAMBARD

Acknowledgements

Many thanks to Marie-Thérèse Dunant-Becker for permission to translate her father's poems and to the editors of *Modern Poetry in Translation* in which one of these translations (*Desire Has No Legend*, 4) first appeared.

I am grateful for a bursary, funded by the Culture 2000 programme, for a residency at the British Centre for Literary Translation in the University of East Anglia to concentrate on this translation.

And to Sylvia for her sense of *le mot juste*.

This edition first published in the UK in 2004 by Flambard Press
Stable Cottage, East Fourstones, Hexham NE47 5DX

Typeset by Harry Novak
Cover design by Gainford Design Associates
Printed in England by Cromwell Press, Trowbridge

Plein Amour was first published in France by Librairie Gallimard in 1954
Republished by La Dérobée in 1997
Republished in *Rien que l'amour (Poésies complètes)*
by La Table Ronde, Paris, in 1997
French text © La Table Ronde 1997
Introduction and Translations © Christopher Pilling 2004

A CIP catalogue record for this book
is available from the British Library
ISBN 1 873226 61 6

Flambard Press wishes to thank Arts Council England, especially
its Translation Fund, for supporting this publication financially

ARTS COUNCIL
ENGLAND

website: www.flambardpress.co.uk

Contents

Love at the Full *(Plein amour)*

The Cover

The painting on the front cover by Kirsty Pilling is a version of Max Ernst's *Le Jardin de la France* and adapted to suit Lucien Becker – the two rivers named being closest to him in his youth. At the age of three, after his father's death, Becker moved from his birthplace, Béchy, to his grandmother's home in Riche on la Petite Seille. After attending primary school at Riche, he went as a boarder to Dieuze on la Seille. It was there that he met his wife Yvonne and there that they returned to live in the year before his death. He is buried in Dieuze where the library now bears his name.

The photograph on the back cover is by Kirsty Pilling and Danial Phillips.

The Poet

Lucien Becker was born into a farming family in Béchy, south-east of Metz in the *département* of Moselle (province of Lorraine), in 1911. He was sent to boarding schools in Dieuze and then Metz, where he and a friend founded an anti-petit-bourgeois group they called 'The Intellectual Underworld'. He had broken with religion at fourteen, the village *curé* putting him out of the church under the gaze of the three-hundred-strong congregation. Although he failed his *baccalauréat* and sold vacuum cleaners before joining the army and serving in Syria, he later attended Nancy University to study law.

In 1935 he passed an exam to become a police superintendent. The following year he married Yvonne Chanot and they went to live in Dieuze. Their daughter, Marie-Thérèse, was born in 1941. Executive police work was to take him to Marseille in 1940, Paris in 1945 and, after two quieter years, Dakar in 1952. In 1955 they were back in Paris where he was appointed to *les Renseignements Généraux* (the security branch of the police force). He retired in 1968, first to Lalande (Yonne), then to Neuilly-sur-Seine for eight years, before returning in 1983 to one of the places of his childhood, Dieuze, where he died in 1984.

While still a teenager, Becker attracted the attention of two prominent literary figures, René Char and the Surrealist André Breton, both of whom published early poems of his. Subsequently he abandoned Surrealism for what he called *'un degré zéro de l'écriture'*, a mode adopted by Albert Camus in *The Outsider* and famously theorised by Roland Barthes. Camus corresponded with Becker to tell him how much he enjoyed his writing, finding it more authentic than anyone else's. At the end of the Second World War, during which he forged documents for the Resistance, Becker moved in Existentialist circles in Paris and, steeped in the intellectual absurdism of the time, published his first two books with a major publisher. His style had become completely different, much barer and more comprehensible. As in *Plein amour* (1954), he found an answer to death and nihilism, the *Nothing to Live For*, as the title of one of his earlier books has it, in the transcendent yet very physical reality of 'love at the full'.

In his later years when he hardly wrote at all (his last published collection, *Summer Without End*, came out from a small press in 1961) and immediately after his death, Becker's poetry suffered considerable neglect, but during the 1990s he was rediscovered by a new literary generation.

The Translator

Christopher Pilling is a poet and playwright as well as a translator. His own books of poems include *Snakes & Girls* (winner of the New Poets Award in 1970) and Foreign Bodies (1992). He has published two collections based on paintings: *The Lobster Can Wait* (1998) and the Matisse-inspired *In the Pink* (1998); one about birds: *Cross Your Legs and Wish* (1994); and one about trees: *Tree Time* (2003). His first play, *Torquemada*, won the Northern Playwrights' Kate Collingwood Award, and two others have been performed at the Theatre by the Lake, Keswick: *The Ghosts of Greta Hall* (written with Colin Fleming, 2000) and *Emperor on a Lady's Bicycle* (2002).

Over the years he has translated a number of poets, mainly French. His first major achievement was a complete translation of Tristan Corbière's *Les Amours Jaunes* as *These Jaundiced Loves* (1995). This was chosen as a Book of the Year by the BBC World Service and by Noel Malcolm in *The Sunday Telegraph*: 'These poems by the forgotten genius Corbière (1845–75), with their mix of fantastic symbolism and street-corner slang, are well-nigh untranslatable. But Pilling somehow manages it, with more than a touch of genius of his own.' In *The Observer* Gavin Ewart wrote: 'If anybody thinks translation is a dead duck, he or she should try Pilling's Englishing of Corbière. It's work like this that redeems the whole concept of translating from one language into another.' John Lucas in *Stand* called it 'a work which nobody who cares about poetry can afford to be without', and for Harry Guest, in *Modern Poetry in Translation*, 'Corbière is fortunate in having in Christopher Pilling a poet who responds with delight to the shocking vigour of the poetry, missing none of the excitement, none of the outrageousness, none of the fun. These translations are masterly.'

Pilling's other major translation, this time with David Kennedy, is of Max Jacob's *Le Cornet à dés 1* as *The Dice Cup* (2000), which was shortlisted for the Weidenfeld Translation Prize in 2001. In *Partisan Review* Renée Riese Hubert commended the translators for convincingly conveying 'the salient characteristics of the prose poems. Their faithfulness to the French text is rendered with elegance and style.' Andrea Bedesch in *Francophonia* also praised *The Dice Cup* as 'a very faithful version which has real presence and the plays on words are brought off to great effect.'

Lucien Becker
(1911–1984)

I

One sunny August day the young Lucien (he was eight or nine) was picking cornflowers in a meadow by a river when he saw a stallion struck and killed by lightning. He thought it had happened to him and stood transfixed for a good ten minutes. It had been meant for him. There was only one cloud in the sky. It was event in its purest state with nothing to precede it. He was struck dumb. He approached. No sign of blood. Then he was picking cornflowers again.

In one poem he sees himself as a spot of earth encircled by death and night, on the bed that's always ready for death. His saving grace is woman. A joyless world is covered by fields and woods and villages, where he is taken over by love at its height, by poems, simple yet strangely compelling, where countryside and village are renewed in the miracle of a woman's flesh.

II

Having been attracted by a selection of Lucien Becker's poems in the enterprising Pierre Seghers series of *Poètes d'aujourd'hui* (no.86, published in 1962), I tried to find copies of any of his three collections published by a major publisher: *Le Monde sans joie* (Gallimard, 1945); *Rien à vivre* (Gallimard, 1947); *Plein amour* (Gallimard, 1954). But, new or second-hand, there were none to be had. No one seemed to have heard of him. Then I spotted one in an antiquarian bookshop in Nice. Either the price pencilled in was a mistake or he must be being sought by cognoscenti. In Paris a year or two later I decided to call at the Gallimard headquarters saying I was thinking of translating Becker (I was) and did they have a spare copy. Eventually I was admitted. They hadn't heard of him, but would look in their stores and let me know. Some time later they informed me that they'd found a copy of *Plein amour* and dispatched it. To America, I assume, as it never reached me. I called again another year and it was after this visit that a copy reached me. I had begun to translate a few from the Seghers selection. Now I decided to concentrate on this one collection. By then the copyright had been transferred to Becker's daughter, Marie-Thérèse Dunant-Becker, called Ritou in the poems. And no one could have been more welcoming and friendly. Would my wife and I join them for lunch? Would I like to see letters her father had received from André Breton and Albert Camus? Interest in Becker's work was growing apace and she was delighted to tell me that La Table Ronde would soon be publishing the Complete Poems. They had agreed to hold back until two small presses had reissued *Passager de la terre* (Voix d'Encre, 1993), the section *Le Désir n'a pas de légende* from *Plein amour* (La Dérobée, 1996) and then a complete *Plein amour* (La Dérobée, 1997), and Voix d'Encre had brought out an unpublished sequence: *Toujours toi* (1995).

III

Born near Metz in Lorraine in 1911, Lucien Becker was the son of a farmer. He was barely three when his father died. Although his mother sold the farm, the land was to remain an essential part of Becker's poetic self, an essential component of his poems. To call Becker poetic belies the down-to-earth nature of the poems. They speak of the every-day world in such a way, though, that objects are seen in a new light. Bottles are themselves and in the reflection of light from their surfaces laughter spurts out. And when it comes to woman, as it inevitably does, for without her Becker is at a loss, her body is lit from within like a field of wheat at harvest-time or the flashing of a river.

> Tu es née sur un ordre de la lumière
> qui partage avec toi ses richesses
> et ton corps s'éclaire de l'intérieur
> comme une moisson ou comme une rivière.

This, the first stanza of a poem which doesn't appear in the Complete

Poems, *Rien que l'amour* (La Table Ronde, 1997), is printed in full, by kind permission of Marie-Thérèse, at the end of this introduction.

By the age of twelve Lucien had read the huge encyclopaedia *Le Petit Larousse Illustré* three times. At seventeen he sent his first poems to René Char who published them in 1929. He'd already read the first Surrealist manifesto. In 1930 André Breton published surrealist poems of his. Then after a gap of seven years he started writing poems again, avoiding rich language and surrealism. *'Je tends à un degré zéro de l'écriture'* ('I lean towards ground zero writing'), he wrote, a mode Roland Barthes was to make much of later (1953) and Albert Camus, who knew Becker's work, was to adopt for most of *L'Étranger* (1942). In the immediate postwar years of his first two collections with Gallimard, Becker mixed in the Parisian world of letters, but felt more and more alone. His poems never raise their voice. He writes of windows, walls, doors, ceilings, bridges, roads, paths, tunnels, corridors, rivers, streams and woman – she is the light that holds the night away, union with her keeps the low sky from falling for good.

Things have such a life of their own that they can be oppressive; even the sky. But the rarefied air of a Mallarmé is too thin to be Becker's element. The Baudelaire of *Spleen*, though (*'Quand le ciel bas et lourd pèse comme un couvercle / Sur l'esprit...'* — 'When the low, leaden sky weighs like a lid on the mind...'), is alive and well-formed in him too. *'L'air pèse comme un meuble...'* ('The air has the weight of a piece of furniture...'), he writes. This sense of the palpable is akin to Antoine Roquetin's sensation in Sartre's *La Nausée*, but for Becker there is no sense of nausea, just a sense of emptiness, a nothing-to-live-for sometimes so strong that he opted for *Rien à vivre* as a title for one of his collections. To match his sense of loss and emptiness, Becker's style can sometimes seem what Jean Rousselot termed 'deliberately monotonous'. Whether his poems have a tendency to turn their backs on prosody or no, when he writes of everyday things he transforms them: they are presented in a matter-of-fact manner which almost cancels the intensity behind them. They stand naked. Offering themselves. Allowing an approach to inner depths. To quote Barthes: 'It's as though the silence of a page is broken in the here and now, the here and now of the writer as he writes the poem, the here and now of the reader as he reads the black script on the otherwise blank page and the here and now of the sense of the words.' It is their very present tense (and tense presence) that typifies Becker's style.

Since *Plein amour* was published in 1954, I wonder whether the situation of France in the wake of a world war could have helped bring on a nihilism which his poems struggle against. War does not appear in his verse, despite the fact that his native Moselle touches Germany and he worked for the Resistance, but he can write:

> Shade is in the trees
> like a hand that's been cut off.

In the long run there is nothing to live for; in the short run there is the tangible world of nature – fields of wheat, streams, pebbles, shadows and grass – and the ordinary world man has built round himself – walls, windows, doors, ceilings, corridors, bridges, paths and roads. And these are the flesh of his poems, keeping death at one remove. By remaking them in language, and setting them in quatrains with lines of unequal length, but lines whose length is dictated by sense and breathing, he forms a patina over what would otherwise be despair, a film over blankness. But that is the point. His verse is not ornament, for ornament is decorative. His language is everyday vocabulary, though not what would be said; his rhythms tend towards the prosaic, but not ones that have been heard before. 'The miracle of *Plein amour* is that the poetry is so full that you don't notice the lack of rhymes. They're not needed.' (Marcel Jouhandeau in a letter to Becker, *Rien que l'amour*, p.364) In fact, several poems do use rhyme, which may pass unnoticed, being such an integrated part of the verse they are in.

He can take into himself images of the visible world and give them a second presence. Things take on such a reality that they are no longer out there in the world. They can even be invasive: 'Insects are crushed in full flight under our skin'. The light in this particular poem is from the eyes of the woman. And when arms and legs intertwine, a burst of sunlight through the trees sinks the very forest into their flesh and sets it on fire down to the last tree. It is such an all-inclusive world that he creates in metaphor – the subterranean river flows within her and her body is the bridge, and the closer they look at one another, the more it is night between them – the night where light must end. He has written a body into existence, only for its transience to shine for the space of a poem.

The plain language may have moved into metaphor, but it's like the pikestaff, somehow still as plain, yet in a different dimension, the only one he can provide against a wordless indifference. A forest can grow from her; in her alone a fire can burn. She is the world transformed, the world as it always was, but renewed; she is as alive as the cry from a fruit that's just been bitten. Her eyes keep him alive and any word must move out from their single body. The act of love is the only place. A timeless one: a stream stops flowing for a moment, the better to be dazzled by the nakedness of the light.

The sexual experience is seen as a phenomenon of the natural world like this, but also as being affected by man's actions. *Le Désir n'a pas de légende* (the title of part two of *Plein amour*) sees desire as having no past, not even an imaginative one, for there can be no legend. It's always present, true fact, true to itself, walled in maybe, where everything is in the picture, no need for a caption (the second sense of *légende*). The tangible world is made visible, audible too, its sound, given body, has body – woman in a room in a poem.

Becker's verse gives death a run for its money, supplying as it does its own coinage, word-objects, presences, and what more present than woman. By calling her up, he gives her substance, emotional as well as physical, and by taking her into his inner world he can create a oneness with her despite the nothingness around. The path he seeks does not go beyond her body. She is the impasse. Through love-making the landscape outside is transformed. The world of nature is so much a part of the sexual experience that nature herself has a tender sensuality:

> The forest does not dare to advance towards the fields of wheat
> for fear of snapping a single stalk.

The titles of sequences of poems in *L'Été sans fin* (his fourth collection, 1961), *Les pierres dans le soleil* and *Le soleil dans les pierres*, confirm the interpenetration of natural phenomena. By naming, Becker recreates the lost land, the things of the earth, the creatures…

The mask most writers can't help wearing may have been thrown off, but the bare style is still a cover for the nothing underneath, omnipresent death only kept at bay by love-making, a unifying but temporary solidity, itself a cover if not a mask, which, fortunately, can be summoned up by closing one's eyes:

> …je n'ai qu'à fermer les paupières
> pour qu'en moi tu prennes la place de la mort.
> *(Les Pouvoirs de l'amour*, 17)

> (I have only to close my eyes
> and you take death's place within me.)

By entering the poem one can be taken out of oneself and assimilated into it or the poem may let itself be assimilated. Then the images stay with us, the readers, their very sensuousness becoming a part of our reason for living: a present fullness.

IV

Claude Vigée writes – justly, in my opinion – 'Becker's poems have a muted sonority, a dull lustre like that of the embers which, on lonely farms on the barren plateaus of Lorraine, continue to glow under the ashes throughout the long winter nights.'

V

The uncollected poem *Tu es née sur un ordre de la lumière* is printed in *Neuf Poètes* (Seghers, 1957) and reprinted (p.89) in *Le Livre d'or de la poésie française contemporaine de 1940 à 1960*, vol.1 (compiled by Pierre Seghers for Marabout Université, 1969), but not in *Rien que l'amour – Poésies complètes* (La Table Ronde, 1997):

> Tu es née sur un ordre de la lumière
> qui partage avec toi ses richesses
> et ton corps s'éclaire de l'intérieur
> comme une moisson ou comme une rivière.
>
> Il ne faut pas que tu aies peur
> dans l'immense bague de l'horizon
> puisque ton cœur peut battre à l'aise
> derrière le seul arbre de mes doigts.
>
> L'amour nous donne alors la force
> de suivre une aventure de soleil
> à l'unique lueur de notre sang
> entre des murs que l'on entend respirer.
>
> Tu entres dans ma vie avec la certitude
> que, menée à deux, elle n'aura pas plus de fin
> que le matin de roche du monde,
> que la nuit surgissant d'entre les siècles.

You were born by command of light herself
who shares her riches with you
and your body lights up from within
like a harvest or a river does.

You mustn't be afraid
in the horizon's huge eternity ring
since your heart can take its ease beating
behind the only tree my fingers can make.

Then love can give us the strength
to go on a sun-bathed adventure
lit only by the glow of our blood
between walls we hear breathing.

You come into my life with the certainty
that, lived together, it will no more end
than will the rock-strong morning of the world,
than will night looming up through the centuries.

This poem, having rhymes in the first stanza, leaves us unfulfilled for they are the only ones. The certainty in the last verse is stressed as if to make up for a lack. When his fingers are seen as a tree, I see them as a multi-trunked hazel, a tree often grown for its fruit. His word for the ring of the horizon is a word for a ring worn on the finger. His walls breathe. And his woman contains the natural world – as in *Plein amour.*

Christopher Pilling
June 2003

PRÉSENCE DU SOLEIL

PRESENCE OF THE SUN

1

L'ombre ne peut sortir du bois
qu'à la tombée de la nuit.
Elle gagne alors sans bruit
les lits couverts de soie.

Dès qu'une lampe s'allume,
elle rentre dans les murs,
s'y referme comme une blessure
qui va saigner dans les vitres.

Elle veille parmi les pierres
à l'affût des vignobles de clarté
que le soir fait jaillir
d'un sol de plus en plus proche du ciel.

Elle demeure au fond des verres
autour d'une étincelle de jour
qu'elle entretient avec amour
pour que demain le monde se lève.

2

Comme sur un signal donné par le vent,
les feuilles partent pour de longs voyages
qui se terminent souvent par l'arrivée
à un arbre qui n'est pas le leur.

Il suffit qu'une goutte d'eau traverse le ciel
pour que toute la clarté la prenne en chasse
parmi les arbres que rien ne peut desceller,
loin du soleil que l'orage laisse voir par-dessus son épaule.

Et la terre pénétrée jusqu'aux pierres
portera son enfant de pluie
jusqu'au moment où les sources
lui feront un grand visage clair.

1

Shadow can only leave the wood
when night falls. So it's at dusk
that it heads soundlessly
for beds with silk coverlets.

No sooner is a lamp lit
than shadow retreats into walls
and shuts itself in like a wound
that will bleed down windows.

Lying in wait among stones
it watches for evening to make
luminous vineyards spurt
from ground that gets closer and closer to the sky.

It lives in the bottom of wine-glasses
around a spark of daylight
which it lovingly fosters
so the world can get up in the morning.

2

As if on a signal from the wind,
leaves set off on long journeys
that often end with their arrival
at a tree which isn't their own.

It only needs a drop of water to cross the sky
for the whole of light to pursue it
through the trees nothing can uproot,
far from the sun the storm lets us see over its shoulder.

And the earth penetrated down to its stones
will be carrying its rain-child
until the moment springs and rivulets
give it a large shining face.

3

On découvre parfois un passant
qui, sans chercher d'où il vient,
se désespère de ne pouvoir faire sien
le visage dont il s'éprend.

On voit des pierres tournant
autour des pas, au cœur des murs,
des pierres sachant que rien n'est sûr
qui se met à vivre de son sang.

La voix se fane hors de la gorge,
car la terre n'a pas assez d'eau
pour faire pousser deux ou trois mots
hauts seulement comme des orges.

4

Pour aller d'un horizon à l'autre,
le ciel suit les mêmes routes d'eau,
pris parfois dans un arbre si haut
qu'il n'en sort qu'à la tombée de la nuit.

Il y a toujours une rose qui pourrit
appuyée contre un mur que le jour
ne parvient pas à trouer pour
y rencontrer l'ombre dont il est épris.

Si l'on colle l'oreille contre les champs,
on entend le bruit que font les racines
pour étreindre le plus de terre possible
sous les forêts d'où naît sans cesse le printemps.

Au soleil en liberté sur les campagnes,
je préfère celui auquel dans ma chambre
il m'arrive en hiver d'offrir un siège
et qui aime, à son départ, que je le raccompagne.

3

You sometimes come across a lone
passer-by, who, without you knowing where
he's from, is so in despair
that he can't have the face he's falling for for his own.

You see stones swivelling where you've stood,
and revolving in the heart of walls,
stones that know nothing's certain, all's
unsure if it starts living on your blood.

The voice out of your throat wilts early
for the earth can't allow enough water to flow
to get two or three words to grow
even as tall as fields of barley.

4

To travel from one horizon to the next
by following the same watercourses, the sky
is sometimes caught in a tree so high
that it only climbs out of it at nightfall.

There is always one rose that's rotting
trellised against a garden wall
the day cannot manage to make a hole in
to meet the shadow it's fallen for.

If you glue your ear to the fields
you can hear the sound the roots are making
to embrace as much earth as possible
beneath the forests where spring is endlessly recreating.

To the sun that's free to range the countryside
I prefer the winter one to whom
I sometimes offer a seat in my room
and who, when he's leaving, would have me join him for the ride.

5

Les fleuves ne sont pas assez longs
pour prendre les mesures du monde.
Au fond de l'homme, le cœur sonde
un sang qui n'a jamais vu de ponts.

Battant toujours pour sa propre perte
comme un oiseau frappé en plein vol,
il sait qu'il n'atteindra point le sol
pour s'y poser, veines enfin ouvertes.

Condamné à n'être qu'une bouée
retenue au milieu d'un vivant
dont personne ne peut lui dire le nom,
il feint d'ignorer le sort auquel il est voué.

6

La main ouverte est l'impasse
où se termine chaque homme.
En la fermant, il fait la somme
d'un néant qui ne laisse pas de traces.

Il ne reste dans son regard
qu'un peu de buée prise pour du ciel,
que l'ombre perdue d'une aile,
ou le reflet des vitres trop souvent traversées.

Les murs reculent devant lui
mais, derrière, d'autres plus épais
se croisent comme des épées
qui font croire que le jour luit.

5

They're not long enough, the rivers,
to measure the world by. But deep
within man his heart will keep
sounding blood that's never seen bridges.

Always beating until it is hit
like a bird struck in full flight,
it knows it will never alight
on the ground, its veins finally slit.

Just like a buoy and condemned
to live in one human being
whose name's not even known to the far-seeing,
it pretends not to know its end.

6

An open hand is an impasse, the place
to which every man will come.
By closing it, he can do the sum
of the emptiness that leaves no trace.

All that remains to his gaze
is what he's taken for sky, a little haze,
the lost shadow of a wing,
or the reflection of windows too often seen through.

All walls back away before
him, but, behind, more solid ones appear
crossing like swords
and making us think daybreak is here.

7

Je suis retenu par le poids d'un village
enfoncé dans le sol jusqu'à des fenêtres
qui ne s'allument qu'à la faveur d'un orage
et où bouge, en attendant, la veilleuse d'une étoile.

Le sommeil est entier sous chaque maison
où il est venu après avoir traversé
des champs dont le silence ne laissait percer
que le cri d'un chien à la recherche de son nom.

On entend les murs vieillir auprès des portes
qui ne s'ouvrent bien qu'au passage des morts
dont toute la vie s'est passée, encordée
à la terre qui va de leur seuil aux plateaux.

8

Des buissons veulent arrêter la route
non loin de sa naissance de pierres.
Mais elle pousse comme un lierre
que la mer seule peut couper.

Un navire alors naîtra d'elle,
reliant tous les sentiers du monde.
Autour de lui, l'horizon
forme enfin le plus pur des cercles,

parce que, dans les blés sans âge,
la route n'a pas su se terminer
sous l'étoffe légère des soirs
où les pas se font au rythme d'un temps mort.

7

I am held down by the weight of a village
buried in the ground up to its windows
which only light up with a storm
and, until one comes, with the pilot light of a star.

Sleep is so sound beneath each house
it has reached after crossing
fields whose silence would only let the yap
of a dog through, a dog barking to hear its name.

You can hear the walls growing old by doors
that only open fully to let the dead through,
those whose whole life was spent, roped
to the land that goes from their front step to the high plains.

8

Bushes want to halt the road
not far from its birth as stones.
But it grows like a limb of ivy
only the sea can cut off.

So a vessel will be born from it
to link all the paths in the world.
Around this vessel the horizon
finally forms the purest of circles,

because, in the ageless cornfields,
the road hasn't known how to come to an end
under the tulle of evenings
where footsteps follow the rhythm of a bygone age.

9

La terre a fait de l'homme
une plante sans racines, ni cime
et il pense sans cesse à l'abîme
vers lequel ses veines rampent.

Pourvu d'un cœur plus tumultueux que la mer,
il doit vivre à l'étroit dans un corps
dont il ne connaît que les bords
et où il se cogne jusque dans ses rêves.

Enchaîné à ses pas, il reste sur place
malgré l'appel amical du couchant
et son désespoir est si grand
qu'il ne peut, même en pleurant, perdre la face.

Il n'a plus que la ressource
de ramener les limites de l'horizon
à celles de son lit où, plomb,
il descend au fond de la plus noire des sources.

10

Avant d'entrer dans les bois,
la pluie frappe aux feuilles
qui sont pour elles le seuil
d'une solitude sans poids.

Elle a parcouru tout l'espace
pour venir sans hâte couler
dans d'obscurs sentiers
où rien ne doit marquer son passage.

Il suffit pourtant d'un rayon de soleil
pour qu'éclate sa présence,
pour qu'un instant la forêt pense
aux vitres dont elle l'émerveille.

Un couchant doit surgir
de cet incendie d'eau
où la terre s'éclaire de ce qu'elle a de plus beau
parce qu'elle aime les forêts à en mourir.

9

The land has made of man
a rootless and topless plant
and he can't stop thinking of the abyss
his veins are slithering towards.

Given a heart more turbulent than the sea,
he must live in the narrow confines of a body
whose edges are all he knows
and they get knocked even in his dreams.

Chained to his footsteps, he is transfixed
despite the friendly appeal from the sunset
and his despair is so great
that he cannot, even by weeping, lose face.

The only resort he has
is to pull in the bounds of the horizon
to those of his bed where, a lead weight,
he pitches to the bottom of the blackest well.

10

Before entering the woods
the rain taps on the leaves
– the first step to achieve
a weightless solitude.

She's crossed the whole of space
to come and flow at last
slowly down dark pathways
where nothing must show she's passed.

Yet just one ray of sun could
make her presence blaze
so that for a moment the wood
will think how window-panes can amaze.

A sunset should suddenly grow
from this forest fire of wet
when the earth lights up with her loveliest show
because she loves the woods to death.

11

Le brasier du jour se débat
comme un fou sur les vitrines.
Dans un verre vide, le miel
du couchant fond à n'en plus finir.

Il faut briser l'écorce des portes
pour trouver le noyau de chaleur
d'où monte, vivant, le bonheur
laissé par quelques belles mortes.

Les carreaux ne peuvent empêcher
la nuit de faire peur à l'enfant
qui va se noyer dans son sang
en rêvant de champs de coquelicots.

12

Ces figurants qui ne veulent pas rire,
forêts, fleuves, roches, céréales,
vivent sans savoir de quel mal
l'homme est atteint depuis qu'il doit mourir.

Les pierres dont l'âge se compte par siècles
ont beau venir à lui en l'entourant de murs,
elles ne lui révéleront jamais rien
des secrets qui les font presque éternelles.

Les plantes se penchent plus volontiers sur son sort
en le poussant sous leurs tunnels de fruits.
Or, même lorsqu'en elles le vent bruit,
elles ne disent pas comment faire pour arrêter la mort.

11

The brazier of day is fuming
like a madman at the window-panes.
In an empty glass, the honey
of the sunset is forever melting.

You must break through the doors' hull
to discover the kernel of heat
and rising from it, full of life, the joy
left by a few beautiful women who have died.

The panes cannot prevent night
giving the child a real fright
and the child will drown in his
blood dreaming of fields of poppies.

12

These extras who do not want to laugh,
forests, rivers, rocks, cereal crops,
live without realising what misfortune
man suffers because he must die.

Stones whose age is counted in centuries
come surrounding him in vain with walls,
but will never give him an inkling of the secrets
that make them almost eternal.

Plants look more kindly on man's fate
ushering him into their tunnels of fruit.
Yet, even when the wind swishes through them,
they don't tell how to stop death in its tracks.

13

Mille oiseaux de lumière fuient vers le couchant
quand le soir abat l'ombre des grands arbres
et posés, non loin des sommets du monde,
ils attendent que les rejoigne le temps.

Certains d'entre eux s'attardent
sur la plus large feuille d'une branche
et la font briller comme un miroir
où pour la dernière fois les insectes se regardent.

Lorsque la nuit sera venue
il sera facile de capturer
tous ceux qui sont restés
au fond des ruisseaux nus.

14

La nuit s'enfle du silence
de toutes les voix mortes
derrière les murs, derrière les portes
où la vie compte encore ses chances.

Le beau temps laisse fondre son or
dans les fruits, dans le miel
se rappelant qu'il est du ciel
dont l'été s'est fait un corps.

Il pourra ainsi en plein hiver
briller au fond des celliers
que la neige vient regarder
du haut de ses arbres de fer.

13

Hundreds of birds of light fly off towards the sunset
when evening fells the shade of tall trees
and, having alighted not far from the world's summits,
they wait for time to catch them up.

A few of them stay on
on the broadest leaf of a branch
and make it shine like a mirror
in which, for the last time, insects see themselves reflected.

When night has come
it will be easy to capture
all those that have stayed
on the bed of naked streams.

14

Night swells with the silence
of all the dead voices
behind walls, behind doors
where life still counts its strokes of luck.

The fine weather lets its gold melt
into fruit, into honey
remembering it's out of sky
that summer has made itself a body.

Which is why in the middle of winter
it can shine deep in wine cellars
that the snow comes to look at
from the top of its iron trees.

15

Le calcaire, neige du plein été,
empêche la terre de saigner
sur les racines qui veillent
et se relaient jusqu'à la mer.

Les cailloux ont mis des années
pour briller comme le soleil
et dans l'herbe ils tendent l'oreille
à l'affût du silence qui règne dans l'éternité.

Si un homme les écrase du pied,
ils font un nid dans la terre
et attendent qu'il soit mort
pour en sortir, plus durs que jamais.

16

Un paysan est pris dans les blés
qui tournent avec le monde
en marquant le pas près des rivières
et sans que rien remue au-dessus de l'été.

Avec la moisson serrée contre lui,
il est seul comme peut l'être
une lumière qui cherche
à sortir de la nuit.

C'est à ce moment qu'il entend
l'appel de ses ancêtres
qui demandent à revivre pour connaître
la paix régnant parmi les céréales.

15

Limestone, snow of full summer,
can stop earth bleeding
onto the roots that stay on their toes
and take over from one another all the way to the sea.

There are pebbles which have taken years
to shine like the sun
and in the grass they cock an ear
for the silence reigning in eternity.

If a man crushes them underfoot,
they make a nest in the ground
and wait for him to die
before they come out, harder than ever.

16

A farmer is caught in the cornfields
that turn with the world
marking time near rivers
when nothing stirs above the summer.

With the harvest clutched tight to him,
he is alone
as a light can be
when it's trying to escape from night.

It's at this moment that he hears
the call of his ancestors
asking to live again to know
the peace that reigns where cereals grow.

LE DÉSIR N'A PAS DE LÉGENDE

DESIRE HAS NO LEGEND

1

Passé le genou où la main se creuse
comme une semence qui germe
en soulevant un peu la terre,
je vais vers ton ventre comme vers une ruche endormie.

Plus haut ta peau est si claire
que les jambes en sont nues pour tout le corps
et mon regard s'y use
comme au plus tranchant d'un éclat de soleil.

Au-delà, il y a ta lingerie qui sert à t'offrir
et à colorer mon désir.
Tes cuisses, lisibles de toute leur soie, se desserrent
et je vois la ligne de partage de ta chair.

Géants de la sensation,
mes doigts vont se fermer
sur le seul point du monde
où se carbonisent des hauteurs entières de jour.

Et c'est enfin la pleine rivière
que je remonte sans effort,
parce que tes seins s'y élèvent
comme deux cailloux à fleur d'eau.

1

Once past the knee where my hand digs in
like a seed pushing up the soil a little
as it germinates,
I move towards your belly as towards a sleeping hive.

Higher up, your skin's so clear and smooth
that your legs are naked with your whole body's nakedness
and my gaze shows such signs of wear
as it would in a sunburst's strongest glare.

Beyond, your underclothes act as an offering of yourself
and to colour my desire.
Your thighs, legible in all their silkiness, unclench
and I see where your flesh divides.

Gigantic with sensation,
my fingers will close
over the only fixed point in the world
where the entire heights of daylight burn to the ground.

And here at last is the swollen river
I sail effortlessly up,
because your breasts stand out in it
like two pebbles on the surface of the water.

2

Dès que tu entres dans ma chambre
tu la fais se tourner vers le soleil.
Le front sur toi de la plus faible lueur
et c'est tout le ciel qui t'enjambe.

Pour que mes mains puissent te toucher
il faut qu'elles se fraient un passage
à travers les blés dans lesquels tu te tiens,
avec toute une journée de pollen sur la bouche.

Nue, tu te jettes dans ma nudité
comme par une fenêtre
au-delà de laquelle le monde n'est plus
qu'une affiche qui se débat dans le vent.

Tu ne peux pas aller plus loin que mon corps
qui est contre toi comme un mur.
Tu fermes les yeux pour mieux suivre les chemins
que ma caresse trace sous ta peau.

3

Le couple que nous formons ne naît bien que dans l'ombre
et, nus, nous allons à la conquête des eaux dormantes
d'où le désir surgit comme un continent toujours nouveau,
à celle des orages qui tombent en nous, lourds et chauds,

à celle de tous les végétaux dont il nous faut,
lèvres à lèvres, briser l'écorce tendue,
à celle des fenêtres dans lesquelles ta chair dérive
comme une jetée qui a rompu son point d'attache.

Parce qu'ils sont les yeux de la terre,
les carreaux se tournent vers ta gorge
qui brille comme un peu de foudre
en regagnant les fonds marins de la ville.

Flanc contre flanc, nous descendons tous deux
dans les souterrains où l'on perd corps
et où les baisers que tu me donnes, que je te donne
sont autant de pas que nous faisons l'un dans l'autre.

2

As soon as you come into my bedroom
you make it turn towards the sun.
Your brow has only to glow faintly
and the whole sky throws its leg over you.

For my hands to be able to touch you
they need to blaze a trail
through the fields of wheat where you are standing
with a whole day's pollen on your mouth.

Naked, you throw yourself into my nakedness
as if out of a window
beyond which the world is nothing more
than a poster flapping in the wind.

You cannot go further than my body
which is held against you like a wall.
You close your eyes the better to follow the pathways
my caresses trace under your skin.

3

We make a couple only fully born in shadow
and, naked, we set out to take over still waters
out of which desire rises like a world that's always new,
to outflank thunderstorms that rain down in us, heavy and warm,

to take on all the trees and plants whose stretched skin
we shall need to break through, with your lips to mine,
to outdo windows in which your flesh goes adrift
like a jetty torn from its mooring.

Given that they are the eyes of the earth,
the window-panes turn towards your breasts
which shine like bolts from the blue
on their way back to the marine depths of the town.

Side by side we go down together
into the subterranean galleries where one loses one's body
and where the kisses that you give me, that I give you
are so many steps we take into each other.

4

Il me faut inventer d'incroyables pièges de chair
pour prendre le monde dans un baiser,
il me faut abattre les murailles dont tu t'entoures
pour que le plaisir puisse te couper en deux.

C'est alors que l'air est dans ma bouche
la racine même de l'espace et des fruits
que, pour me laisser passer de ma vie à ta vie,
tu te fais arche des épaules aux pieds.

Partout sur les murs, sur les visages
la lumière se dévêt de sa lingerie
et montre son beau ventre de femme
d'où l'ombre tombe comme une fourmilière écrasée.

Car il y a vraiment de quoi vivre sur la terre,
mais il faut avoir la force des arbres
pour pouvoir repousser le ciel bas
que la mort fait peser sur les paupières.

5

L'espace est pris entre nos regards
et nous n'avons que quelques gestes à ébaucher
pour qu'il tombe à nos pieds sans faire plus de bruit
que la dernière goutte d'eau d'un orage sur la forêt.

Tu es plus nue sous mes mains
que la pluie sur les tuiles,
qu'un feuillage dans le matin,
que les dents ensoleillant la bouche.

Des insectes s'écrasent en plein vol sous notre peau,
mes doigts ne cherchent pas à se protéger de la lumière
qui s'élève du fond de tes yeux
pour faire se lever dans les miens un jour insoutenable.

Le reste de notre vie se fige autour de nous
en hautes statues qui ne peuvent entrer
dans le cercle de silence et de joie
qui nous serre aux reins.

4

I have to invent incredible flesh-traps
to catch the world in a kiss,
I have to smash down the walls you build around yourself
so that pleasure can cleave you in two.

It's only then that air is, in my mouth,
the very root of space and fruit;
that, to let me move from my life into yours,
you arch yourself from your shoulders to your feet.

Everywhere on walls, on faces
light divests itself of its underclothes
and shows its beautiful woman's belly
from where shadow falls like a crushed anthill.

For there are very good reasons for living on earth
but what we need is the strength trees have
in order to push it back up, the low sky
that death has pressing on our eyelids.

5

Space is trapped between the looks we exchange
and we have only to move a little
for it to fall at our feet with no more sound
than the last drop of water from a storm over the forest.

You are more naked beneath my hands
than the rain on the roof-tiles,
than leaves first thing in the morning,
than the teeth that are the sunshine of your mouth.

Insects in full flight are crushed under our skin;
my fingers don't try to protect themselves from the light
rising from the depth of your eyes
to make a day dawn in mine that's so hard to prolong.

The rest of our life solidifies around us
in tall statues which cannot enter
the circle of silence and sensual delight
that squeezes our bellies together.

6

Enlacés par l'herbe que l'air fait monter jusqu'à nos lèvres,
nous oublions dans notre chambre les paysages
qui venaient vers nous au pas de la terre,
les beaux paysages qui nous prenaient pour des statues.

Vagues s'en allant à la rencontre l'une de l'autre,
nos corps n'ont que la flaque des draps
pour apprendre que l'amour est une montagne
qui s'élève à chaque coup de reins.

Nous n'avons que nos bras et nos jambes
pour serrer un instant les forêts
qu'un éclat de soleil enfonce dans notre chair
et fait flamber jusqu'au dernier arbre.

Nos dernières paroles se sont arrêtées loin de nous,
enfin coupées de leur tronc de sang.
Nous entrons seuls dans un monde ouvert sur nos visages
comme sur son propre noyau.

7

Je cherche dans ta bouche la source
du fleuve souterrain qui te parcourt
en rejetant en haut des cuisses
son écume de plante fraîchement coupée.

Quand tu écrases ton ventre contre moi,
quand mes doigts aiguisent ta gorge,
tu as des mots doux comme la salive,
des mots qui auraient poussé après un orage.

De ton corps je fais un pont
qui me conduit dans un monde
où nos dents se cognent contre le même verre d'air,
où nos regards à force d'être proches font la nuit entre eux.

Je ne vis plus au jour le jour
puisque tes baisers font partie de mon avenir
et nous allons jusqu'au bout de la lueur
que la foudre trace en remontant nos veines.

6

Entwined by grass that the air raises to our lips
we forget, up in our room, the landscapes
which came towards us at earth-pace,
the beautiful landscapes that would take us for statues.

Waves rolling to meet one another,
our bodies have only the tarn of the sheets
to learn that love is a mountain
rising with every thrust of our loving.

We have only our arms and legs
with which to squeeze for a moment the forests
a brilliant shaft of sunlight buries in our flesh
and sets it alight down to the very last tree.

Our final words have halted at a distance from us,
chopped off at last from their trunk of blood.
Alone we enter a world as open on our faces
as it is at its centre.

7

I search in your mouth for the source
of the subterranean river that flows through you
and throws out above your thighs
its froth like a freshly-cut plant.

When you crush your belly to me,
when my fingers sharpen your breasts,
you say words as sweet as saliva,
words which must have grown after a storm.

From your body I make a bridge
that leads me into a world
where our teeth knock against the same glass of air,
where our eyes, with being so close, make night between them.

I no longer live from day to day
since your kisses are part of my future
and we are going to the far end of the bright glow
lightning traces as it forks up our veins.

8

Il me suffit de quelques gestes pour retrouver,
enfouie sous ta peau, la plante nue que tu es
et, vacillant de tout le soleil conquis par les ruisseaux,
tu entres dans la nuit avec le jour devant toi.

Je n'ai qu'à toucher la pointe de tes seins
pour que soient soudain rompues les mille écluses
qui retiennent entre nous un poids d'eau égal à celui de la mer,
pour que toutes les lumières s'allument en nous.

Et quand dans la clarté du drap,
tu n'es plus qu'un éventail de chair,
j'ai hâte de le faire se refermer sur mon corps
par une caresse que je jette en toi comme une pierre.

9

En te renversant sur le lit,
tu donnes à la clarté la forme même de tes seins
et le jour use toute sa lumière
à vouloir ouvrir tes genoux.

Tu prends ta source dans le miroir qui coule du mur,
tu as du soleil jusqu'au fond de la gorge,
tu es neuve comme une goutte de rosée
que personne n'a vue, que personne n'a bue.

Tu as le cou fragile de ces oiseaux
qu'on voit rarement se poser sur la terre
et quand tu es dans la rue le regard des hommes
monte autour de toi comme une marée.

8

I only need to feel you a little to discover,
tucked under your skin, the naked plant you are
and, flickering with all the sunlight the streams have tamed,
you enter the night with the day ahead of you.

I only have to touch the tips of your breasts
for a thousand lock-gates to suddenly burst open,
gates that keep a weight of water between us equal to the sea's,
for all the lights to come on in us.

And when in the brightness of the sheets,
you are nothing more than a fan of flesh,
I hurry to make it close over my body
with a kiss that I throw into you like a pebble.

9

As you throw yourself backwards onto the bed
you give light the very shape of your breasts
and day wears out all its iridescence
in its urge to part your knees.

You rise in the mirror that flows from the wall,
you have sunlight down to the depths of your throat,
you are as newfangled as a drop of dew
no-one has seen, no-one has drunk.

Your neck is as vulnerable as the necks of those birds
one rarely sees landing on the ground
and when you are out in the street men's gaze
comes up around you like a tide.

10

Derrière tes dents, ta chair commence
avec ses aubépines de fièvre et de sang.
Tu sais qu'elle est une prison
dont mon désir te délivre.

La caresse fait son bruit de poumon
en cherchant dans tes cuisses
le papillon qui s'y est posé,
presque fermé en toi de ses ailes.

Avec l'aveuglement d'une taupe,
tu creuses l'air de tes seins.
Autour d'eux mes mains s'élèvent
comme une montagne coupée en deux.

11

Tu m'accueilles dans un pays au centre duquel
ton corps se dresse comme un feu de joie,
simplement posé sur la fraîcheur de tes lèvres
au point où l'espace se jette en toi.

Tu es l'impasse vers laquelle j'accours
avec la force des marées,
avec la liberté des moissons
qu'un coup de faux sépare du soleil.

Nous ne parlons pas de l'amour qui nous lie
parce qu'il est entre nous comme une bouteille sur une table
et qu'il court de mes doigts à tes doigts
avec la vitesse de l'éclair.

10

Behind your teeth, your flesh begins
with its hawthorns of fever and blood.
You know it's a prison
from which my desire delivers you.

My kiss is a big intake of breath
as it delves between your thighs
for the butterfly that's alighted there,
its wings almost enclosed in you.

With the blindness of a mole
you hollow out the air with your breasts.
Around them my hands rise up
like a mountain cleft in two.

11

You welcome me to a country at whose centre
your body stands like a beacon,
simply placed on the freshness of your lips
where space throws itself into you.

You are the blind alley I rush towards
with the strength of tides
with the freedom of harvests
that the sweep of a scythe cuts off from the sun.

We don't talk of the love that binds us
for it's here between us like a bottle on a table
and it leaps from my finger-tips to yours
at the speed of lightning.

12

Si je veux t'aimer sans rien perdre de ta clarté,
je suis contraint de m'enfermer avec toi dans les pierres.
Le jour écarte de temps en temps les rideaux,
tache ton épaule et retombe dans la rue.

Le silence même est fait de minéral
et prend la forme des chambres qui le contiennent.
Pour qu'il n'y entre point, c'est mille armoires
qu'il aurait fallu pousser contre les portes.

Notre nuit est imperméable et nos corps,
se suffisant de l'air contenu dans un baiser,
descendent jusqu'aux racines de l'arbre
qui a nos têtes pour sommet.

13

En plein front, en plein flanc,
j'entends les pas que mon sang fait
pour s'avancer de sommet en sommet
jusqu'à celui dont il me faut dominer ton corps.

Je lui en veux de me tenir enfermé
dans un visage avec lequel je reste si seul
lorsque mes épaules n'ont plus le tien à porter
et que je te cherche en vain dans les miroirs.

C'est pourtant par lui que je t'ai reconnue dans la rue
dans un moment qui reste comme une source en pleine mémoire.
C'est lui qui me permet à chaque instant
de reconnaître ma vérité dans tes yeux.

12

If I want to love you without losing any of your brilliance
I am constrained to shut myself away with you in the stones.
Daylight draws the curtains from time to time,
tarnishes your shoulder and falls back into the street.

The very silence is mineral
and takes on the shape of the bedrooms that contain it.
To stop it entering, hundreds of tallboys
would have to have been pushed up against the doors.

Our night is watertight and our bodies,
making do with the air contained in a kiss,
go down to the very roots of the tree
that has our heads as its crown.

13

Full on my forehead, full on my ribs,
I hear the pad pad pad of my blood
climbing on from summit to summit
up to the one where I have to tower above your body.

Which is exasperating for it keeps me enclosed
in a face with which I remain so alone
when my shoulders no longer bear the weight of your face
and when I vainly search for you in mirrors.

And yet it's by your face that I recognised you in the street
in a flash, an inspiring one, still so vivid in my memory.
It's what allows me at every instant
to recognise my truth in your eyes.

14

Tu ouvres la nuit la plus pleine
de la pointe de tes seins.
Tu viens vers moi dans le tournoiement d'une ville
qui ne s'éclaire plus qu'à la clarté du désir.

Je ne saurai jamais la distance à parcourir
entre la lampe sourde de ton ventre et mon corps.
Je sais que je te rejoins dans un baiser
qui ne laisse point passer le jour.

Sous ma main ensablée dans les caresses,
il reste les hauteurs de ta gorge,
vers lesquelles j'avance,
la bouche pleine de soleil.

A force d'avoir mon visage contre ton visage,
j'oublie que le monde commence au-delà de ton regard.
A jeter l'un dans l'autre nos plus sûrs filets,
nous ramenons tous les poissons de la joie.

15

Le soleil se couche dans les flaques
pour rester plus longtemps sur la terre.
Tu ne peux plus t'en aller de ma chambre
parce que je suis debout sur tes derniers pas.

J'essaie de conquérir
l'insecte que tu respires.
Mais il s'échappe de mes lèvres
pour aller se poser sur mon sang.

Tu ne peux plus sortir du filet
que mes mains tendent sur toi,
tu es au centre de l'étoile de mes pas,
tu es l'unique réponse de ma vie.

14

You open the most sumptuous night
with the points of your breasts.
You come towards me in the whirling of a town
lit from now on only by the bright lights of desire.

I shall never know the distance there is to travel
between the dark lamp of your entrance and my body.
I do know that I join you in embraces
that do not let daylight through.

Beneath my hand choked with sand in caresses
all that's left are the heights of your breasts
towards which I advance,
my mouth full of sunlight.

By having my face close up to yours
I forget that the world begins beyond your gaze.
By casting our safest nets one inside the other
we harvest all the fish of rapture.

15

The sun beds down in puddles
wanting to stay longer on earth.
You can't leave my bedroom any more
for I'm standing where you last stepped.

I try to quash
the insect you breathe.
But it escapes from my lips
to settle on my blood.

Now you can't escape from the net
my hands pull over you,
you are at the centre of the star my steps make,
you are my life's single answer.

16

A nos regards pris dans la même pierre de présence,
le monde arrive par une fenêtre
où nous nous penchons parfois
de nos corps, hauts comme des promontoires.

La ville est au pied de la chambre où tu te tiens
avec pour horizon celui de tes épaules
et nous touchons jusqu'en son fond
le vivier de feu qui donne sa mesure à l'été.

Tu te refermes sans cesse sur moi
comme deux vagues sur un rocher
et nous n'avons qu'à nous laisser porter par la mer
qui s'étend très loin autour de nos visages.

Perdus dans un pays de chair et de caresses,
nous vivons les quelques milliers d'années
dont notre amour a besoin pour que naisse
une étreinte de chaque goutte de notre sang.

17

Je suis prisonnier de ton visage
à la façon dont un mur l'est du miroir.
Pesé par ton regard,
le monde perd son poids de pierres.

Le chant de ton sang sous la peau
est aussi doux à entendre
que celui des graminées
poursuivies par le vent.

Je sais que la mort ne peut rien me faire
tant que tu restes entre elle et moi,
tant que s'allume dans ta chair
le ver luisant du plaisir.

Le couchant tournoie sur chacun de tes ongles
avant d'aller grossir la terre d'une dernière montagne de clarté
et je peux voir à ton poignet les pas
que ta vie fait pour venir jusqu'à moi.

16

To meet our gazes held in the same stone of presence,
the world comes in through a window
we sometimes lean out from
with the whole of our bodies, high up here like promontories.

The town is at the foot of the room you're in
with your shoulders for its horizon
and we touch the very bottom
of the fiery fish-tank which wants to show summer its prowess.

You constantly close over me
like two waves over a rock
and we've only to let ourselves be carried by the sea
that stretches out and away from our faces on every side.

Lost in a country of flesh and caresses,
we live the few thousand years
our love needs for a passionate embrace to be born,
squeezing every drop of our blood.

17

I am a prisoner of your face
as one wall is of the mirror.
Weighed by the look you give,
the world loses its burden of stones.

The song of your blood under your skin
is as sweet to hear
as the song of grasses
pursued by the wind.

I know death can do nothing to me
so long as you stay between it and me,
so long as the glow-worm of pleasure
keeps coming alight in your flesh.

The setting sun eddies on each of your fingernails
before it goes to swell a last mountain of brightness
and I can see by your wrist the steps
your life is taking to reach me.

18

Au-delà de mes mains refermées sur toi,
au-delà de ce baiser qui nous dénude,
au-delà du dernier mot que tu viens de dire,
il y a le désir que nous tenons vivant contre nous.

Il y a la vie des autres qui remonte de la ville
sans pouvoir aller plus loin que la porte
derrière laquelle les murs écoutent à notre place
le bruit que le cœur des hommes fait dans la rue.

Tu dépasses les herbes
de quelques hauteurs de soleil.
Je te sens à peine bien que je sois sur toi
comme sur la pointe la plus aiguë d'une montagne.

Tu es entière contre chacune de mes mains,
tu es entière sous mes paupières,
tu es entière de mes pieds à ma tête,
tu es seule entre le monde et moi.

19

Le soleil reste sur ta bouche
à la place où miroite encore un baiser.
Ton visage lui appartient mais il me le rend
pour des nuits plus longues que ma vie.

Ton corps pour lequel je m'éveille
s'éclaire plus vite que le jour
parce que le soleil surgit à toutes les places
où il y a des cailloux à pétrir.

Les forêts se dénudent pour lui
dans le secret de leurs clairières
mais c'est sur ta gorge
qu'il fait pousser ses plus beaux fruits.

La terre lui présente une à une
ses vallées les plus riches,
mais c'est sur ton ventre qu'il s'arrête,
simple bouquet de flammes.

18

Beyond my hands closed on you,
beyond this kiss stripping us bare,
beyond the last word that you've just spoken,
there is desire that we keep alive by hugging it to us.

There is the life of other people coming up from the town
but unable to get further than the door
behind which the walls are listening in our stead
to the sound the hearts of men make in the street.

You are several sun times
higher than all the grasses.
I can barely feel you although I'm on top of you
as on the sharpest point of a mountain.

You are whole against both my hands,
you are whole beneath my eyelids,
you are whole from my head to my foot,
you are alone between the world and me.

19

The sun stays on your mouth,
on the spot where a kiss still sparkles.
Your face belongs to the sun, but he returns it to me
for nights longer than my life.

Your body for which I wake
grows light quicker than day does
because the sun comes out
wherever there are pebbles to knead into shape.

The forests bare themselves for the sun
in the secret of their clearings
but it's on your chest
that he grows his loveliest fruits.

The land offers him one by one
her most opulent valleys,
but it's on your belly that he alights,
a simple bouquet of flames.

20

Le toit des villages est posé sur la terre
et les prés fuient de toutes parts
autour des murs blancs
qui avancent d'une maison par siècle.

Je pense à l'étonnement de ton ventre
qui regarde toujours mon désir pour la première fois.
Je pense aux forêts que nous faisons tomber
quand ma chair mûrit dans la tienne.

Je pense à la hauteur de l'été
sur la poussière des routes,
au ruisseau qui s'arrête un instant de couler
pour mieux s'éblouir de la nudité de la lumière.

A rester debout dans ce pays démesuré de clarté,
je sens que je n'ai pas assez de poumons
pour retenir la vie qui vient vers moi
à la façon dont ton corps vient vers le mien.

20

The roof of the villages is placed on the ground
and the meadows rush off in all directions
around the whitewashed walls
which advance by one house per century.

I think of the astonishment of your middle eye
which always sees my desire for the first time.
I think of the forests we bring crashing down
when my flesh ripens in yours.

I think of the height of summer
on the dust-laden roads,
of the stream that stops flowing for a moment,
the better to be dazzled by the nakedness of light.

Standing in this enormous floodlit country,
I sense I haven't breath enough
to hold onto the life that comes towards me
in the very way your body comes to mine.

LES DIMENSIONS DU JOUR

THE DIMENSIONS OF THE DAY

1

Les mots ont été créés pour qu'en fermant les yeux
je puisse venir à toi sans faire un mouvement.
Ta gorge s'éveille quand je l'appelle
d'une voix qui en connaît avant moi la forme.

Quand tu n'es pas à portée de mon regard,
quelques mots toujours pareils te remplacent.
Mais je puis aller jusqu'au bout de toi
sans en prononcer un seul.

Dans mon sommeil je te prépare
pour t'avoir plus nue chaque jour.
Je ne suis pas l'esclave de ce que je te dis
parce que chaque parole te délie de mon désir.

Mais ta bouche ordonne les mots dont j'ai besoin
pour être chaque matin dans la rue
l'homme qui va à son travail
avec une tête différente de celle des autres passants.

2

Le vent veut faire éclater la ville
en jetant ses vagues et les forêts qu'il décime
contre les maisons qu'il prend pour des rochers,
contre les fenêtres où pas un rideau ne bouge.

Un volet s'ouvre et se rabat sans cesse
comme un oiseau qui tente de voler.
Tu serres ta jupe contre tes cuisses
de peur de n'être plus qu'un blanc noyau de chair.

Les hommes encouragent le vent presque de la voix
pour que ton corps soit nu bien au-delà de son linge.
Il a toute sa bouche sur toi et elle accède à ta peau
en un baiser qui te porte comme un fleuve.

Tu as la force de m'appeler pour te défendre
mais les mots que tu dis ont le poids
de ceux que du fond de nos étreintes tu laisses monter
comme des bulles de feu qui auraient traversé la mer.

1

Words were created so that when I close my eyes
I can come to you without moving a muscle.
Your breasts wake up when I call to them
in a voice that knows their shape before I do.

When you are out of my sight
a few words – always the same – take your place.
But I can go to the very depth of you
without pronouncing a single one.

In my sleep I get you ready
so I can have you more naked each day.
I'm not the slave of what I say to you
because each word I speak frees you from my desire.

But your mouth commands the words I need
to be every morning in the street
the man on his way to work
with an expression unlike anyone else's.

2

The wind wants to shatter the town
by hurling its waves and the woods it decimates
against the houses it takes for rocks,
against the windows where no curtain stirs.

One shutter swings open and goes on flapping
like a bird attempting to fly.
You hold your skirt tight against your thighs
for fear you might end up as little more than a white nub of flesh.

Men almost shout encouragement to the wind
to have your body naked, completely out of its underclothes.
It's got its whole mouth on you and meets your skin
in a kiss that transports you like a wide river.

You have the strength to call on me to defend you
but the words you speak are as lightweight
as those you conjure up from the depth of our embraces
like bubbles of fire come all the way from over the sea.

3

Avant de disparaître derrière la forêt
le soleil se presse contre ta joue
et nous sentons à peine le lien
qu'il serre autour de nos baisers.

La chambre se jette toute nue
dans le bûcher des vitres
et un dernier arbre de clarté
se couche en travers de ton corps.

L'ombre qui sort des murs
arrive au sommet des collines
d'où elle retombe sur la moisson
qui déborde encore des vallées.

Il ne reste que l'éclat des rivières
et celui, plus sourd, que retiennent tes cils:
c'est de là que chaque jour le matin part
pour aller voir le soleil naître dans les blés.

4

Chaque jour à la même heure
tu t'abreuves longuement aux vitrines.
Tu peux garder tout le soleil sur tes seins
et il peut toucher tes dents comme un fruit.

Tu es pour mes sens le seul objet
sur lequel ils s'exercent complètement.
C'est contre toi que ma caresse devient tranchante
et que mon corps recouvre ses vraies dimensions.

Tu peux ensoleiller toute une chambre
avec la seule clarté qui bat sur ton ventre
au moment où plus rien ne te relie à la terre
qu'un baiser, qu'une étreinte, qu'un regard.

Pour te dépouiller de ta nudité,
pour que le plaisir te traverse dans toute ta longueur,
il faut mettre à jour les diamants que tu as sous la peau
et les tailler jusqu'à ce que le matin en jaillisse.

3

Before it disappears behind the wood
the sun snuggles up against your cheek
and we scarcely feel the bond
it tightens round us when we make love.

The bedroom throws itself completely naked
into the bonfire in the window-panes
and a final tree of brilliant light
is laid across your body.

The shadow coming from the walls
reaches the top of the hills
and falls back on the harvest
still overflowing from the valleys.

All that's left is the rivers' flashing
and the softer glow from under your eyelids:
it's where the morning starts from every day
to go and see the sun being born in the cornfields.

4

Each day at the same time
you quench your thirst with a long drinking in at the windows.
You manage to keep all the sun on your breasts
and it can touch your teeth like a fruit.

You are the sole object for my senses
as I am completely obsessed with you.
It's on you that my caress makes its mark
and there that my body recovers its true dimensions.

You can light up a whole room
with just the sunlight beating on your stomach
and then nothing can keep you earthbound any more
except a look, a kiss, a passionate embrace.

To slough off your nakedness,
so that pleasure may travel the whole length of you,
you must show the diamonds you have beneath your skin
and cut them till morning can sparkle with them.

5

Sur ton corps lisse de caillou
mes mains vont, forêts en liberté,
comme vers des sommets d'où je retombe,
source altérée de soleil.

Ton cœur est si proche de mon cœur
que nos artères se mêlent les unes aux autres
et ne retrouvent plus à nos fronts qu'une seule tempe
pour faire battre l'espace.

Bateau venu de la haute mer,
je vais très loin au fond de tes plages
et je me renverse dans les fougères
qui naissent de ton corps entr'ouvert.

Lorsque nous n'avons plus pour respirer
que l'air écrasé dans nos baisers,
le jour qui nous sépare a beau faire,
il n'arrive pas à être aussi nu que toi.

6

Le soleil avant de se coucher dans les carreaux
atteint sur la table la lame d'un couteau.
Les autres objets sont là, autour de lui,
à attendre la lueur qui va les faire respirer.

Le soleil se retire des champs
après avoir brisé ses lampes dans les ruisseaux.
Pour les garder longtemps au-dessus du monde
les immeubles se font hauts comme des falaises.

C'est l'heure où l'on marche sur la terre
comme sur une passerelle,
où sans te reconnaître tu te regardes dans les vitrines
que rien ne peut tout à fait éteindre.

C'est l'heure où les pierres s'endorment au fond des vallées
tranquilles comme des bateaux amarrés,
où je peux fermer les yeux jusqu'au matin
sans qu'en moi l'ombre monte autour de ton souvenir.

5

Up over your body, pebble-smooth,
my hands move, free forests ranging
as if to hilltops from which I fall,
a beck thirsting for sunlight.

Your heart is so close to my heart
that our arteries mingle
and find our foreheads now but a single temple
for space to throb in.

Boat in from the high seas,
I pull across your beaches, press on inland
and lie back in the bracken
that's born from where your body opens.

When all we have left to breathe
is the air crushed in our kissing,
the daylight that keeps us apart tries in vain
to be as naked as you.

6

Before it sets in the window-panes, the sun
reaches the blade of a knife on the table.
The other objects are there, around it,
waiting for the gleam that will give them the breath of life.

The sun withdraws from the fields
after breaking its lamps in the streams.
To keep them for as long as possible above the world
the blocks of flats make themselves as tall as cliffs.

It is a time for walking the earth
as if it were a gangplank,
for not recognising oneself in shop-windows,
a reflection nothing can completely extinguish.

It is a time for stones to fall asleep, deep in the valleys,
tranquil like boats at their moorings,
a time for me to close my eyes till morning
with no shadow growing round my memory of you.

7

Je m'éclaire longuement avec l'or
que je trouve au fond d'une étreinte.
Enhardis par tant de lumière,
nous dénoyautons le soleil dans un baiser.

La ville voudrait que le ciel parte de ses murs,
la ville voudrait aller au-devant des chemins,
qui s'arrêtent dans les champs de céréales
mais elle reste enfoncée dans le sol comme un tiroir.

A force de rejeter les objets dans leur passé,
je n'ai plus, comme point d'appui, que ta bouche
et nos visages sont si près l'un de l'autre
que tes yeux se ferment presque avec mes paupières.

Une lampe suffira pour marquer la place
où le jour s'est ouvert le front.
De loin dans la nuit on verra s'élever
son grand buisson d'orties blanches.

8

Dans les trains que les gares tirent
à bout portant sur la nuit,
dans la chambre où nous nous brûlons
au plomb fondu de l'amour,

dans la rue où tu passais tout à l'heure
en faisant descendre le ciel jusqu'à toi,
dans les mains qui ne peuvent déchirer
les dernières affiches du plus beau des couchants,

dans l'espace qu'on voudrait tirer à soi
pour le contraindre à s'ancrer quelque part,
dans les paroles lancées comme des amarres
qu'autour de nous rien ne peut retenir,

il y a toujours le même miroir où la vie regarde
sans savoir pourquoi les pas qu'elle entend décroître
sont ceux d'un être qui n'existe plus
que par les gestes que lui permet ton amour.

7

I am alight for ages with the gold
I find in the depths of our loving.
Made bold by so much light,
we suck the sun's kernel out with a kiss.

The town would like the sky to leave her walls,
the town would like to run and meet the roads
that come to a standstill in the cornfields
but stays stuck in the ground like a stuck-fast drawer.

What with pushing objects back into their past
all I have to rely on is your mouth
and our faces are so close to one another
that your eyes almost shut with my eyelids.

A lamp will be enough to mark the spot
where day split its forehead open.
From far off in the night we shall see
its huge clump of white dead-nettles rising.

8

In the trains which stations shoot
point-blank at the night,
in the bedroom where we burn each other
with the molten lead of love,

in the street where you were walking just now
bringing the sky right down to you,
in the hands which cannot rip away
the final displays of the loveliest of sunsets,

in space one would like to pull into oneself
to oblige it to anchor itself somewhere,
in the words thrown out like mooring ropes
that nothing around us can restrain,

there's always the same mirror where life is watching,
not knowing why the footsteps it hears growing fainter
belong to a creature which no longer exists
except in the gestures your love allows.

9

Du soleil il ne demeure que quelques étoiles
qui tournent lentement avec le ciel
et le jour pour lequel l'univers n'était pas assez grand
se laisse capturer dans les lampes.

De toi je ne discerne plus qu'une épaule
comme un couchant au bord du drap,
qu'une tempe où, telle une source,
le sang fait remuer ses herbes les plus hautes.

Mais tes yeux fermés sont les bourgeons
d'où va surgir deman toute la forêt
et la voix que tu gardes, posée sur tes lèvres,
donnera, en me nommant, un nom au silence.

La nuit continue à marcher de son pas de géant
sur chaque semence de la terre,
sur ta gorge vissée à fond dans mes mains,
sur le rêve où nous allons nous rencontrer.

10

L'été devient le plus grand poisson
que peuvent contenir les ruisseaux.
L'été devient le plus haut cristal
que nous pouvons porter à deux.

De ma tête au point culminant de l'air,
il n'y a que la distance d'un mètre de lumière
avec lequel je cherche à mesurer l'être
qui va et vient de mon visage à ton visage.

Les chemins s'avancent vers moi
comme les branches d'un arbre
qui aurait pour racine l'endroit
où tu poses les pieds.

Dans la forêt, nous marchons sur la clarté
comme sur des serpents domestiqués
mais le soir ils s'enfuient sous le pont
que le couchant jette sur son propre fleuve.

9

All that's left of the sun are a few stars
that turn slowly with the sky
and day, for which the universe was not large enough,
lets itself be captured by the lamps.

All I can discern of you is a shoulder
like a sunset at the sheet's edge,
and a temple in which, like spring-water,
the blood makes its tallest grasses sway.

But your closed eyes are the buds
from which the whole forest will sprout tomorrow
and the voice you keep to yourself, out on your lips,
will give, by naming me, a name to the silence.

Night continues striding like a giant
over every newly-sown crop,
over your breasts my hands have screwed down tight,
over the dream in which we shall be meeting.

10

Summer is becoming the biggest fish
the streams can contain.
Summer is becoming the tallest rock-crystal
we two can carry together.

From my head to the air's zenith
there's only one metre's length of light
with which I try to measure the creature
that's to-ing and fro-ing from my face to yours.

The roads advance towards me
like the branches of a tree
that has as its root the very spot
where you place your feet.

In the forest, we walk on bright light
that feels like house-trained snakes,
but in the evening they slide away beneath the bridge
the setting sun casts over its own river.

11

Mes mains cherchent sur toi la place
où ma caresse fait son bruit de soie
et nos corps se tiennent debout avec, contre eux,
le poids des murs de toute une ville.

D'un seul regard, d'un seul baiser,
je suis plus près de ton corps que tu ne le seras jamais
et ta bouche vient se poser sur la mienne
un peu comme l'écume au-dessus d'un ruisseau noir.

Il suffit que je te prenne dans mes bras
pour qu'entre nous surgisse un essaim
dont nous pressons la grappe chaude
à l'endroit où nous sommes hauts d'un seul sommet.

12

Personne ne pense au village
qui n'est plus qu'un œuf écrasé.
Le soleil est entier sur chaque tuile
et jamais le calcaire n'a souffert d'une telle soif.

Il y a des souterrains de verdure et de fraîcheur
dans l'été où les routes sèchent jusqu'à la pierre,
mais on ne les découvre qu'à la tombée du jour
à l'heure où les ruisseaux recommencent à couler,

à l'heure où la nuit n'a plus pour s'éclairer
que la lampe sourde des moissons
à l'heure où tu es prise dans le couchant
comme un bel objet dans une vitrine.

11

My hands seek out the part of you
where my stroking makes its silky sound
and our bodies stay standing with the weight
of a whole town's walls against them.

With a single look, with a single kiss,
I am nearer your body than you will ever be
and your mouth alights on mine
a little like the froth on a dark stream.

I only need to take you in my arms
for a swarm to surge up between us
and we press its warm cluster
to the place where we're a single summit high.

12

Nobody's thinking of the village
that's nothing now but a squashed egg.
The sun is wholly on each tile
and never has chalk suffered such a thirst.

There are underground passages, cool and green
in summer when roads dry down to the stone,
but you only discover them at nightfall,
that hour when streams start to flow again,

that hour when night has nothing else for light
but the muted lamp of harvests,
that hour when you are caught in the setting sun
like a beautiful object in a shop-window.

13

A tourner entre ces murs gris
que sont tous les visages,
le ciel ne prend sa vraie couleur
qu'au-dessus de ton front.

L'espace se veut plante sans fruits
pour ta bouche qui tient le jour,
pour ton regard qui cherche en moi
quelque chose de plus clair que la lumière.

Les carreaux font les maisons plus larges
avec, à fleur de verre, des têtes
que rien ne peut rattacher aux corps
dont elles ne cessent de dire le nom.

Mais il reste le miracle de ta présence
au milieu des paroles que nous prononçons
pour que l'amour ait la hauteur des montagnes
qui s'ouvrent, chaque matin, sur le soleil nu.

13

With spinning round between these grey walls,
every one a face,
the sky only assumes its proper colour
above your forehead.

Space really wants to be a plant with no fruit
for your mouth which holds the daylight,
for your look which seeks in me
something brighter than light itself.

The window-panes make the houses wider
and there on the glass are heads
nothing can attach to the bodies
whose names they never stop saying.

But there's still the miracle of your presence
in the midst of the words we utter
so that love can have the height of mountains
opening, every morning, to the naked sunlight.

LES POUVOIRS DE L'AMOUR

THE POWERS OF LOVE

1

Les objets aident le jour naissant
à aller à la rencontre de ton regard
et ils reprennent aussitôt leurs visages
de témoins d'un monde sans profondeur.

Pour communiquer les uns avec les autres,
ils ont tout un alphabet de reflets
et dès que tu franchis le seuil de ma porte
ils te montrent la place qu'ils t'ont gardée près de moi.

Ils ne peuvent partager notre existence
mais à travers leurs doigts mal joints
ils s'étonnent parfois de découvrir qu'à deux
nous pouvons ne plus former qu'un seul objet.

2

La chambre qui ne cesse le jour de s'étendre
à la faveur de continents mal démasqués
ne va plus maintenant au-delà des murs
dans lesquels elle est prise comme un front.

La terre s'arrête un moment de tourner,
prise entre les genoux des grands fleuves,
emmêlée dans les vols d'oiseaux
qu'elle organise de village à village.

De mon cœur, exerçant son métier de vivant,
s'élève un feu qui ne sait brûler qu'en toi
mais nous n'en voyons que l'étincelle
dont tes tempes s'allument et s'éteignent.

1

Objects help the breaking day
to come and meet your gaze
then straight away they resume their faces,
witnesses to a world with no depth.

To communicate with each other
they have a whole alphabet of reflections
and no sooner do you come through my door
than they show you the spot they've kept for you near me.

They cannot share in our existence
but through their slightly parted fingers
they are sometimes astonished to discover that the two of us together
can be but a single object.

2

The bedroom, which by day can't stop stretching
out to whole continents yet to be properly unveiled,
stays now within the walls
that hold her tight like a forehead.

The earth stops turning for a moment
held between the knees of the wide rivers,
entangled in the flights of birds
which she directs from village to village.

From my heart, carrying on with its job of living,
leaps a fire which can only burn in you
but we only see the spark of it
whenever it lights up your temples or goes out.

3

Entre le monde et la nuit
il y a l'épaisseur d'un carreau
à travers lequel la lumière va surgir
pour se jeter dans celle de tes yeux.

Au ras du sol, les feuilles se lissent
pour recevoir le soleil
qui passera de l'une à l'autre
en allumant le brasier de la rosée.

Tes paupières battent comme les sources
dont le matin veut éveiller la terre,
les oiseaux s'immobilisent un instant
pour mieux sentir la rondeur de la clarté.

Et c'est le jour porté de colline en colline,
renversé dans les lits de la verdure,
c'est le jour éperdu de joie
dès qu'il reconnaît tes seins.

4

Comment sortir de notre chambre,
prisonnière du sommeil,
sans pouvoir oublier la veille
de ce jour que rien n'enchante,

de ce jour mesuré
comme un litre de lait,
de ce jour dont le front
cherche un regard sous les ponts?

Il faut s'accrocher à même le sol
pour éviter les trous de nuit
par lesquels le jour fuit
sans jamais jouer son rôle.

Je dois longtemps scruter les glaces
pour voir s'élever ta vie ou l'été
vers des hauteurs de clarté
que, seuls, tes yeux dépassent.

3

Between the world and the night
there is the thickness of a window-pane
through which light will suddenly surge
to cast itself into the light of your eyes.

On the ground, leaves sleek themselves
to receive the sun
which will travel from one to the next
stoking the dew's brazier.

Your eyelids palpitate like the springs
morning wants to waken the earth with;
the birds stay still for an instant
the better to sense the roundness of light.

And it is daylight borne from hill to hill,
thrown down onto beds of grass,
it is daylight overcome with delight
the moment it recognises your breasts.

4

How can we leave our room, a
prisoner of sleep,
without having to keep
memories of the day before yesterday

when everything palled, measured
out like a litre of milk – a dud
of a day for a forehead which is
out to catch someone's eye under bridges?

You'll need to hold onto the ground hard
to avoid the holes of the night
through which daylight is put to flight
without ever playing its part.

I must stare into mirrors a long time
to see your life or the summer rise
towards the radiance which your eyes
alone can rise above and outshine.

5

Je ne sais que faire de mon regard
loin de la ville qui agrandit ma vie,
loin de toi sans qui mon désir se dépayse
et si bouleversante quand tu te mesures à ma nudité,

loin des vitrines dont le soir se sert
pour mettre autour de toi le plus fervent des halos,
loin des réverbères qui contemplent, avec moi, tes yeux,
loin du bruit qui couvre celui de mon cœur.

Le soleil a beau peser sur les sources
de tout son poids d'étoile vivante,
les herbes attendront l'hiver avec la patience
que met parfois la pluie à noyer l'horizon.

C'est à peine si certains fruits sourient
quand, mûrs, ils se laissent cueillir,
c'est à peine si les arbres se retournent
quand je fuis le village scellé dans l'été.

6

Loin des villages caillés, loin des routes
qui courent voir le soleil se lever sur les usines,
nous descendons dans l'été
comme au fond d'une cloche sous-marine.

Avec le cœur remonté jusqu'à la mort,
nous laissons le ciel se souder à nos yeux.
Je tiens ton visage dans ma main ouverte
comme s'il était ma seule richesse.

Ton regard, lourd de cils, est si mince et si long
qu'il est facile à ma vie d'en faire son horizon.
Avec tout le poids de l'espace sur la nuque,
tu viens, d'un seul baiser, te délivrer sur ma bouche.

Il nous faudra des années
pour revoir l'oiseau de clarté
qui se jetait chaque matin dans la vitre
et qu'on retrouvait, tué, le soir en plein miroir.

5

I don't know what to do with how I see things
away from the town which enlarges my life,
away from you without whom my desire is disorientated
and so overwhelming when you match yourself to my nakedness,

away from the shop-windows evening uses
to surround you with the most fervent of haloes,
away from the street lamps that gaze, with me, into your eyes,
away from the noise drowning the beating of my heart.

The sun weighs down in vain on the source of rivers
with its whole living weight, its heavenly body weight;
the grasses will wait for winter with the patience
rain sometimes has when it drowns the horizon.

Certain fruit hardly smile at all
when, ripe, they allow themselves to be picked;
the trees hardly turn to look
when I run away from the village sealed in summer.

6

Far from the clotted villages, far from the roads
running to see the sun rise over the factories,
we go down into summer
as if we were going deep into a submarine bell.

With our hearts wound up to the point of death,
we let the sky weld itself to our eyes.
I hold your face in my open hand
as if it were my only valuable.

Your look, heavy with lashes, is so narrow and long
that it's easy for me to make it my life's horizon.
With the whole weight of space on your nape,
you come, with a single kiss, to give yourself up on my mouth.

We shall have to wait years
for another sighting of the bird of light
that used to hurl itself every morning into the window
and we would find dead in the evening in the full face of the mirror.

7

Adossé à l'ombre comme à un contrefort,
je vois les maisons se noyer dans les fenêtres
et la plaine recommence à faire tourner son disque
entre les bords enfin visibles de l'horizon.

Les paysages sont figés dans la verdure,
loin des villes que je ne peux quitter
parce que mes pas sont inscrits d'avance
dans toutes les rues où ma statue bouge.

Ton regard, trop grand pour l'espace,
fait de moi un être
à la recherche d'un chemin
qui ne va point au-delà de ton corps.

Tu es la seule chose
que je puisse tenir contre moi
et tes yeux d'amour sont uniques
comme le plus beau des couchants de mon enfance.

8

Le soleil est dans les pierres
comme une statue renversée.
L'ombre est dans les arbres
comme une main coupée.

Les villages sont blancs
dans le cercle bleu de l'été.
Les insectes qui poursuivent le jour
se tuent dans les vitres.

Tu es seule à savoir faire rire les cailloux
qui glissent sous la verdure comme des poissons
et les ruisseaux essaient en vain
de voir au travers de la terre.

Nous nous arrêtons dans les moissons
et l'univers s'arrête en même temps que nous.
Nous sommes sûrs qu'aucun chemin n'a pu nous suivre,
que la mort même a perdu notre trace.

7

Leaning back against the shadow as if it were a buttress
I see the houses drowning in the windows
and the plain start once more to spin its disc
between the edges of the horizon we can see at last.

The landscapes have congealed in the greenery
far from the towns I cannot leave
because my footsteps are already imprinted
in all the streets where my statue moves.

The look of you, too big for space to contain it,
makes of me a being
on the lookout for a pathway
that goes no further than your body.

You are the only thing
I can hug to me
and your eyes, so full of love, are unique
like the most beautiful sunset of my childhood.

8

The sun is in the stones
like a statue that's been knocked down.
Shade is in the trees
like a hand that's been cut off.

The villages are white
in the blue circle of summer.
The insects in pursuit of daylight
kill themselves on the window-panes.

You are the only one who can make the pebbles laugh
as they slip under the grass like fish
and the streams try in vain
to see right through the earth.

We come to a standstill in the fields being harvested
and the universe stops there and then.
We are convinced no road could have followed us,
and that death itself has lost our tracks.

9

Le jour commence à reconnaître les fenêtres
avant de s'avancer sur la terre
dans les tessons de la rosée,
parmi les cailloux qui veulent te voir, nue.

Dans la chambre où tu dors,
il trace une presqu'île de clarté,
haute seulement de ta gorge dénudée
et d'un visage d'où tu dois éclore.

Le soleil passe à travers ta lingerie
comme si elle était le plus pur des nuages.
Il y demeure jusqu'au moment
où elle reprendra la forme de ton corps.

Tu attends qu'il se couche sur toi
pour le serrer contre ton ventre
et, lorsque tu lui en ouvres les bords,
il devient bleu dans tes yeux.

10

Enfermé dans un horizon sans altitude,
je n'ai devant moi que chemins en fuite
vers un lointain de plus en plus illisible,
de plus en plus tourné sur ton absence.

J'attends en vain que vienne à ma rencontre
un arbre qui marcherait sur ses racines,
mais c'est à peine s'il me fait signe
en remuant un bras d'où quelques feuilles tombent.

Les fleurs sourient d'une façon si banale
qu'il me tarde quand je reviens à la nature
de la quitter pour la ville où je suis sûr
qu'un seul de tes baisers me bouleversera jusqu'à la moelle.

Il reste les couchants dont je ne puis me déprendre
parce qu'ils ont brillé au-dessus de mon enfance
comme mille mains levées sur un navire en partance
pour un pays que tu es seule à savoir me rendre.

9

Before advancing on the earth
daylight begins to recognise the windows
in the shards of dew,
and among the pebbles which want to see you, naked.

In the room you sleep in,
it traces a clear peninsula of light
that only comes as high as your bare breasts
and a face you must blossom from.

The sun passes through your underclothes
as if they were the most innocent of clouds.
It pauses there until
they take on the shape of your body again.

You wait for it to lie down on you
so you can squeeze it to your belly
and, when you open up to it,
it becomes blue in your eyes.

10

Enclosed by a level horizon
all I have before me are roads that fly off
towards a more and more illegible distance
that's more and more turned in on your absence.

I wait in vain for a tree to come and meet me,
one that can walk on its roots,
but it scarcely ever so much as waves
an arm at me, an arm from which a few leaves fall.

The flowers smile in such a trite way
that, when I go into the country, I can't wait
to get back to town where I'm convinced
a single one of your kisses will shake me to the core.

There remain the sunsets – so much a part of me
because they have shone over my childhood
like hundreds of hands waving goodbye from a ship setting sail
for a country you alone know how to return.

11

Tes cheveux se dénouent sur mon corps
comme une moisson de blé perdue
au détour d'un champ de rosée
dans un matin qui n'a pas de bords.

Tu cherches mes lèvres avec la soif
de quelqu'un qui a traversé le monde
pour aller voir la neige fondre
sur des sommets moins hauts qu'un baiser.

Tu es vivante comme peut l'être
le cri d'un fruit qu'on mord.
En t'aimant, je prends tout l'or
qui veille à l'entrée de ta chair.

12

Les fenêtres regardent passer
le long serpent d'hommes
qui entre dans les pierres
avec, devant lui, le silence à traverser.

Le monde peut se refermer sur nous
de ses plafonds, de ses tuiles,
nous devenons gigantesques et invulnérables
parce que nous sommes un instant maîtres du désir.

Il y a tes lèvres, plantées d'air pur,
tes dents comme du soleil en pleine source,
tes yeux qui me font rester au niveau de la vie,
il y a la parole se séparant de notre chair.

11

Your hair falls loose over my body
like a harvest of wheat lost
on the way round a field of dew
on a morning that has no edges.

You seek out my lips with the thirst
of one who has crossed the world
to see the snow melt
on summits not as high as a kiss.

You are as alive as the cry
of a fruit can be when it's bitten into.
By loving you, I take all the gold
that watches over the entrance to your flesh.

12

The windows watch them going past,
men, the long snake of them
entering the stones
with, ahead, the silence to cross.

The world can close in again on us
with its ceilings and its tiles,
but we become gigantic and invulnerable
because we are, for an instant, masters of desire.

Here are your lips, sown with pure air,
your teeth like sunlight at its source,
your eyes keeping me down in this world,
and there's the word separating itself from our flesh.

13

Aucun des mots ne peut s'user
que j'emploie pour nommer mon amour
et ta bouche en relève sur ma bouche une trace
qui se décalque à travers nos baisers.

Je calme la lueur sourde de ton ventre
comme le soleil une tempête
et je me retrouve toujours avec une tête
unie à la tienne par-dessus des siècles de mort.

Nue jusqu'à laisser voir ton cœur
dans la transparence de ses battements,
tu n'as plus contre moi pour limites
que celles d'un jour sans terre à éclairer.

Je veux sceller au tien mon visage
afin que je puisse mourir en toi
au moment où il ne restera autour de moi
que le ciel grand ouvert de ton regard.

14

La nuit se couche au bord des routes
comme un grand chien très doux
et tu cherches à apaiser les étoiles
en les prenant dans tes cils.

Les montagnes qui avancent avec l'ombre
stationnent au-dessus des arbres
à qui elles font toucher le ciel
sans qu'aucun de leurs fruits ne tombe.

Seul, le ruisseau continue à couler,
heureux enfin d'être entendu des herbes
et de pouvoir aider la terre à tourner
à l'intérieur du silence.

A la place où ton sommeil
devient mince comme du verre,
un rêve s'inscrit en lettres
qui éclairent l'étendue de mon sang.

13

Not one of the words I use to name my love
has a chance of wearing out
and your mouth picks up a trace of them on my mouth
through our kissing.

I calm the muted glow of your belly
like the sun can calm a storm
and I still keep finding my head united
with yours, joined above centuries of death.

So naked you've let your heart be visible
in the transparency of its beating,
you no longer have any boundaries to keep me out
except those of a day with no earth to light.

I want to seal my face to yours
so I can die inside you
precisely when all that's left around me
is the wide open sky of your gaze.

14

Night beds down by the roadside
like a big cuddly dog
and you try to soothe the stars
by taking them into your lashes.

The mountains, advancing as shadow,
come to a standstill above the trees
which they oblige to touch the sky
without a single fruit falling.

Only the stream continues to flow,
pleased at last to be heard by the grass-blades
and able to help the earth turn
deep within silence.

In the very place where your sleep
becomes thin as glass,
a dream inscribes itself in letters
that light up the whole span of my blood.

15

Les lampes mesurent l'étendue de la nuit
et font briller au passage ton regard
d'un éclat qui entr'ouvre l'ombre
dans laquelle le monde va nous enfermer.

Des bassins de clarté gisent au fond des vitres
d'où le soleil n'a pu se retirer à temps
et la rivière qu'il parcourt dans sa longueur
jaillit des ponts qui la serrent à la gorge.

Lorsque la nuit a tiré, l'une après l'autre,
les poignées d'alarme des visages,
la rue s'arrête de marcher entre ses berges
et je ne suis plus contre toi qu'une forme blanche.

Les lampes deviennent autant de vivants,
morts en gardant les yeux ouverts
sur une ville où ton souffle est le seul rythme
qui convienne au silence.

16

Il me faut aller vite dans tous les sens
parce que partout autour de moi
des femmes qui vont mourir se donnent
à des hommes dont la mort est pour demain.

Je dépense sans compter l'or de l'amour,
je goûte à ton corps comme à un verre
dont je n'ai pas le temps d'achever le contenu
parce que j'ai la main de la mort sur la gorge.

Il importe peu que je dise mon nom
à celles que je rencontre sur la route:
ma mort n'aura pour témoin que le visage
dont j'aurai vécu de tout mon regard.

15

The lamps measure the extent of the night
and, as you pass, make your look shine
with a brilliance that opens up the shadows
in which earth will enclose us.

Pools of bright light lie in the depths of the windows
the sun has not withdrawn from in time
and the river whose length it travels down
spurts out from the bridges that seize it by the throat.

When night has pulled fistfuls of fright,
one after the other, out of people's faces,
the street stops walking between its banked edges
and I am nothing more now than a white shape against you.

The lamps become so many living beings,
dead from keeping their eyes open too long
to look on a town in which your breathing is the only rhythm
that suits the silence.

16

I have to go fast in every direction
because everywhere around me
women who are going to die are giving themselves
to men whose death is for tomorrow.

I spend the gold of love without counting,
I taste your body as if it were a glass of wine
whose contents I haven't time to finish
because death's hand is at my throat.

It doesn't much matter whether I say my name
to the women I meet along the way:
my death will have as its only witness
the face I have lived in with all my seeing.

17

Le plafond devient noir
au-dessus de mes yeux pourtant ouverts
et je te devine encore dans l'ombre
qui te serre contre moi.

Le sang lèche une dernière fois
mes tempes de sa flamme bleue.
Il vient de quitter mes lèvres,
vissées maintenant à fond sur le silence.

Les murs qui s'épaississent dans ma mémoire
vont-ils s'écrouler sur la seule présence,
ta présence, que je veux emporter
jusqu'au bout de ma pensée?

Mais j'ai tant refait ton visage avec mes mains,
j'ai tellement inscrit ton nom sur ma bouche
que je n'ai qu'à fermer les paupières
pour qu'en moi tu prennes la place de la mort.

17

The ceiling is turning black
above my eyes which have stayed open
and I guess you're still there in the shadows
which are holding you tight against me.

Blood is having a last lick
at my temples with its blue flame.
It has just left my lips,
screwed hard down now on silence.

Will the walls thickening in my memory
crumble at the very presence,
your presence, that I want to carry off with me
to the far end of my thoughts?

But I have remade your face so often with my hands,
I have inscribed your name so often on my mouth
that I have only to close my eyes
for you to supplant death inside me.

AFTERWORDS

Various French writers, particularly poets, wrote to praise Becker for his achievement. I have chosen the following extracts from letters published in La Table Ronde edition of his Complete Poems, where they clearly refer to poems in *Plein amour*.

Gaston Bachelard

I really like your Universes which have a loved woman at their centre, these worlds that spin round the fingernail of a white hand. And how you know how to live! How you sense the dialectic of walls that protect us and shut us in. Stone has both these aspects for you. Everything becomes sensitive under your gaze. ... It's time to bring metaphorical light to life, the flash of lightning you find 'in a deep embrace'. In this way you possess the personal dimension of luminous day. You do your job of living so well that, old philosopher that I am, I have a renewal of life reading you. (1954)

René Char

Your poems are good companions. They are clear-sighted, well considered and, when night comes, all their words put themselves to bed with us. The objects they have named expose their freshness, their perfect good sense. That's harmony. (1954)

Léopold Sédar Senghor

I started to read your new collection in the plane bringing me back to Paris and I read to the end as it absolutely delighted me. I won't hide what I think. I consider you at present to be one of the greatest love poets in French. What I love in your poems is that you always transcend the image and the senses to reach the idea that exists in the anguish of what it is to be human. And what language! I admire the fact that you can, with simple words and without adjectives, sing a song that can touch us so deeply. (1954)

Georges Mounin

You communicate in a voice that's yours alone, one you've had more or less from the start. It never seems to come from carefully applying rules of language or prosody laid down in advance. This voice, your indelible mark, has this about it, it engenders poems of such a sameness, that it's extremely hard to single out a single line, a single verse, even a single poem more typical or more perfect than all the others. There's a poignant monotony, always on the move before our eyes, like water passing. (1958)

What pleasure finding your look and your voice again, however pained. They don't lie. What deliverance, next to so many puffed up blabbings that take themselves for poetry. (1961)

Jacques Réda

Your poems always have that unpolished sound and obstinate movement that makes them unique. I don't see poetry as just something to be read, but a violent intermittent need very few contemporary poets can satisfy and you've been one of them for some considerable time. (1961)

*

If there's an element of monotony in Becker, I hear it, as René Ménard does, having an effect similar to that of Gregorian plainsong. For Marcel Jouhandeau (1955) the miracle of *Plein amour* is that the poetry is so present that the absence of rhyme goes unnoticed. There is rhyme here and there, but Becker did say that rhyme is more harmful than useful and observed that it played a few tricks on Baudelaire even.

I'd also like to quote from letters by Lanza del Vasto and Jean Tardieu, because they strike me as getting to the nub of Becker's verse.

Lanza del Vasto

I love the extreme spareness of your style, the poverty of the language, the versification that doesn't shine but has no flaws and, as each line turns, at every hemistich even, an image that pins an idea into our flesh, that inserts itself into us with a push of a fingernail. I'm putting your manuscript among the few things I like to keep and keep returning to. (1941)

I find your new verses have the same discreet and penetrating beauty as before. Your poetry has a remarkable unity of tone without being monotonous. Monotony is excluded, despite the external uniformity, because each moment is felt and each word touches the skin. (1943)

Jean Tardieu

What enormous pleasure your poetry has given me! I am impressed by these poems so deliberately free of ornament and graces, and by the seriousness I take to be one of the vital qualities of a poet.... A poem by you is not just a succession of well chosen lines but a whole, an object, or rather, an expression of the spirit, upheld by a secret dialectic. What a great enterprise, wanting to create from everyday life with everyday words poetry that's so moving and purifying! But it's the only sort that, or so it seems to me, suits our times ... with no literary references and nothing false or conventional about it. This is poetry for here, for now, the only kind, because of this, that will last beyond today. (1943)

*

Finally, some words by Lucien Becker himself:

To look at, the world is rather a slippery thing. With the help of one's hands, one has to rediscover its oceans and its mountains, or, even more so, all it contains. Man, beneath the tall stones of towns, is a wood louse. He needs to be shown the sun, which, despite appearances, is far from being a sun of joy. It is woman, woman alone, who is this sun of joy. One has to get burnt by it, thinking all the time that the word LIFE is shorter than the word MINUTE. It's by metaphysical, as well as of course by physical, practice, in response to this unique requirement, that one can rise above one's feet on the ground. (Interviewed by Pierre Béarn, 1951)

As for art, I don't know it. And man I only know through woman... (Interviewed by H. Rode, 1956)

I'm living in the present, either planting beans or going off walking in an endless summer... As for writing, I have no more to say. My desire to write has only been held by a thread. (Letter to Georges Mounin, 1966)